MY LIFE IN 2055

MY SCHOOL IN 2055

CARRIE LEWIS AND CHRISTOS SKALTSAS

Lerner Publications ◆ Minneapolis

Lerner Publications Company
An imprint of Lerner Publishing Group, Inc.
241 First Avenue North
Minneapolis, MN 55401 USA

For reading levels and more information, look up this title at www.lernerbooks.com.

Main body text set in Mikado a Light
Typeface provided by HVD Fonts

Library of Congress Cataloging-in-Publication Data

Names: Lewis, Carrie, 1973- author. | Skaltsas, Christos, illustrator.
Title: My school in 2055 / Carrie Lewis, illustrated by Christos Skaltsas.
Description: Minneapolis : Lerner Publications, [2021] | Series: My life in 2055 | Audience: Ages 7-11. | Audience: Grades 2-3. | Summary: "In the school of the future, children might use tech such as interactive screens, holo projectors, and virtual reality to set their own pace and make learning personalized"– Provided by publisher.
Identifiers: LCCN 2020023889 (print) | LCCN 2020023890 (ebook) | ISBN 9781728416311 (library binding) | ISBN 9781728423555 (paperback) | ISBN 9781728418544 (ebook)
Subjects: LCSH: Schools–Juvenile literature. | Education–Effect of technological innovations on–Juvenile literature. | Educational change–Juvenile literature.
Classification: LCC LB1513 .L48 2021 (print) | LCC LB1513 (ebook) | DDC 371–dc23

LC record available at https://lccn.loc.gov/2020023889
LC ebook record available at https://lccn.loc.gov/2020023890

Manufactured in the United States of America
2-53286-49198-5/2/2022

TABLE OF CONTENTS

REAL OR IMAGINARY?

Let's take a look at the future of schools.

People are always coming up with ideas about how we can help children learn.

Future schools might look like the ones in this book—but then again, they might not!

While you are reading, pause and think about what you've read. What would your school of the future be like?

SCHOOL

WELCOME TO OUR SCHOOL!

This is our school. It's very busy!

Our school is partly underground. It grew as more children came to the city. We had to make more space and the only place to go was down.

Some parts of the school roof are curved and covered with grass. This is so that children can walk, play, and climb on top of the school as well as around it. The grassy roof also keeps the building warm.

LET'S FIND OUT SOME MORE ABOUT SCHOOLS IN 2055.

SCHOOLS ARE OPEN ALL DAY!

In 2055, everyone lives in cities and our schools fill up. Some schools are open from seven in the morning to seven at night, but don't worry—no one goes the entire time!

We go to school in two shifts. The first group starts at seven in the morning and goes home at one in the afternoon. The second group starts at one in the afternoon and stays until seven at night.

Many children and parents like this schedule! It allows families to choose the times that work the best for them.

Most people live close to school and choose to walk. Others cycle or ride a hover scooter to school. This can be fun, but you have to be careful not to go too fast.

Some older kids fly to school with their jet packs—but they need a special license to operate them.

Usually, the first thing we do when we get to school is play sports or go to a dance class. This gets our circulation moving and helps us concentrate.

LEARNING IS PERSONAL

Teachers begin by finding out what students are good at and what they like. This is called personalized learning. It helps everyone succeed.

When we start school at age five, we learn to play together and build our social skills. Later on, we learn reading, writing, and math.

As we get older, we work more independently. Teachers guide us and assign work. If we don't want to work in the classroom, we can go to the library or somewhere that's more comfortable for us.

We don't use paper though, only tablets. The teacher can still check our work because our tablets are linked.

WE LEARN ABOUT THE FUTURE AND THE PAST

We learn the same things you do, but we also have some new subjects.

Teachers tell us about technology and how to use it. We even learn how to make our own technological discoveries.

In history, we learn from the past. We look at things that went wrong and try to understand how to stop them from happening again.

In 2055, our knowledge of space is changing every day. Astronauts are on their way to Mars for the first time. As they pass through space, they send a lot of new information. It's an exciting time to be learning about space in school. We look at new photographs of planets, comets, and stars.

WE LOVE SCREENS

Screens help us learn. We have interactive tablets and headsets so that we can learn at our own speed. These devices are really helpful when we work from home.

The teacher sets the work, checks it online and explains anything that we need help with. This means that we can focus on the areas where we need help.

In 2055, we know that not everyone learns in the same way. Some people learn by watching, some learn by listening and some learn by doing things with their hands.

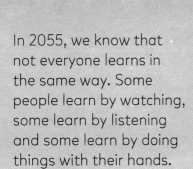

The school has a library, but most of the books are e-books!

We sit in circles so that we can all see the hologram projector in the center.

Ash Cloud

Vent

Crater

Lava Flow

Magma

The hologram projector is a great way of bringing subjects to life. If the teacher wants to show us a human heart, she can bring up a 3D, life-size human body and show us the heart. She can show us other things as well, like a model of a volcano.

If we've been good, the teacher rewards us with 3D movies or games on the hologram projector!

WE CAN GO VIRTUALLY ANYWHERE

Everyone in our class has a VR (virtual reality) headset. When we put these on, we can explore all kinds of places together.

From our classroom, we have visited a jungle, the Arctic, and even Ancient Egypt. There is no better way to learn about a time or place than to feel as if you are really there.

VR has a lot of uses. Younger groups use it to learn how to solve arguments between friends or comfort a friend that is upset. Older groups use VR for practice interviews and job training.

VR headsets can be really useful in a national emergency, like a pandemic, when we have to work from home. It means we can still be with our teacher, our friends, and our class when we are apart.

COMFORT IS IMPORTANT

We've all seen pictures of schools in the old days with rows of children sitting in hard chairs at desks. Our classrooms are nothing like that!

It's important that we are comfortable at school. This keeps us focused and ready to learn. We still sit at desks, but most of the time we are in soft chairs, like beanbags or armchairs.

None of our schools have uniforms. We pick out comfortable clothes so that we aren't distracted.

WE LOOK AFTER OUR BODIES AND OUR MINDS

Even in 2055, there is no magic way to keep our bodies healthy. We have to exercise.

At school, we play team games like soccer to help with our concentration and coordination.

We also have a gym with treadmills and rowing machines to build endurance. If we want to, we can use these with VR.

We know that exercise is good for our minds too. Most people play a sport as a way to help them reduce stress and tension.

We also have a weekly yoga session where we do deep breathing and learn how to calm our minds.

No more soggy mashed potatoes for us! In our school, everyone has a meal that's just right for them.

When we arrive at the cafeteria, we press our thumb to the sensor, and then our food is put on the counter with our name on it. Each person has their own meal.

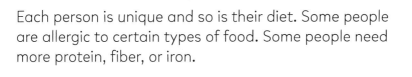

Each person is unique and so is their diet. Some people are allergic to certain types of food. Some people need more protein, fiber, or iron.

In school, we eat in a way that helps us to concentrate on lessons all day. For some people, this might be some eggs and a salad. For others, it might be rice or pasta.

OH YES—WE STILL MISBEHAVE

Kids will always be kids. In 2055 we still get it wrong sometimes.

When someone misbehaves, the teacher helps them understand what they did wrong. This means understanding the consequences of their actions. Was someone hurt because of what they did? Was someone upset? This helps us to develop empathy with other people.

Teachers help kids use social emotional skills to understand their behavior. This often gets to the root of the problem.

There are still some punishments. If you make a mess, then you might be asked to clean up or fix what you did. This helps us all do better.

OUR SCHOOL IS LINKED TO EVERYWHERE

In 2055, the world is an interconnected place. There are huge, global companies with an office in every country.

Our schools are linked too. We don't just have classmates in our own school. We have classmates all over the world! We can take Mandarin Chinese language lessons with our friends in China, or learn how to make beautiful rice flour art with our friends in India.

We love to play together. Many schools have international games clubs, where children can play board games like chess with people on the other side of the world. Sometimes we play games with friends in Brazil!

Being international helps us to understand who we are and what we all have in common with children around the world.

THAT'S PROBABLY THE BEST LESSON OF ALL.

GLOSSARY

consequences
The results of a particular action.

empathy
Understanding the feelings of other people.

global
Something that is all around the world.

personalized
Something that is designed just for one person.

social emotional skills
The ability to connect with other people.

unique
One of a kind.

VR (virtual reality)
Using devices, like a headset, that makes it appear that you are somewhere else.

yoga
Exercises originating in India, aimed at building a strong body and mind.

LEARN MORE

If you want to know more about technology of the future, here are some places to start.

Johnson, Steven. *How We Got To Now*. New York: Viking, 2018

How Stuff Works Website
https://www.howstuffworks.com/

London Science Museum Website
https://www.sciencemuseum.org.uk/objects-and-stories/everyday-technology

National Geographic Website
https://www.nationalgeographic.co.uk/cities-of-the-future

Science Kids Website
https://www.sciencekids.co.nz/technology.html

Smithsonian Website
https://www.si.edu/Kids

INDEX